POWERS OF PSALMS: MANIFESTATION SECRETS USED BY SUCCESSFUL PEOPLE TO CREATE A SUPERNATURAL

AND SUCCESSFUL LIFE

BY

EDIN RINN

Copyright © 2021

All rights reserved under the international and Pan-American copyright conventions. No part of this book may be reproduced or transmitted in any form or by any means, electronic or mechanical, including photocopying, recording, or by any information storage and retrieval system, without permission in writing from the copyright owner.

WARNING!

The formulas in this book are meant to be used only for positive or good intentions.

Do not use them for negative purposes to cause evil in the lives of others. If you do, it would boomerang back to you, a hundred times stronger.

Please, use the formulas only for the good of humanity.

Walk in love and you will attract tons of love in return. There is enough good for you and the rest of humanity.

If you enlarge your capacity to love, you will be the most powerful, prosperous and influential person in your community.

All Bible quotations are taken from the King James version.

This book is based on the research, experience and mystical beliefs of the author. No responsibility is assumed by the author, publisher of vendor for the outcome of experimentation with the information in this book. No claim or guarantee of supernatural, cosmetic or therapeutic effect can be made in accordance with Federal, State and local laws and regulations.

DISCLAIMER AND LEGAL NOTICE

Efforts were made to insure that the information contained herein was relevant at the time of this writing. The author and publisher make no representation or warranties with respect to the accuracy, applicability, fitness, or completeness of the contents of this book. The information contained in this book is strictly for educational and entertainment purposes. Therefore, if you wish to apply ideas contained in this book, you are taking full responsibility for your actions. There is no guarantee that your life will improve in any way using the techniques, ideas, and information presented in this book. Self-help and improvement potential is entirely dependent upon the person using the ideas and techniques. Your level of improvement in attaining results depends on the time you devote to developing your skill, commitment to learning the ideas, techniques, principles, and skills mentioned, and your personal belief system. Spirituality and energy work are faith-based systems, meaning if you do not believe in your own power to effect change, change is unlikely to occur. Since these factors differ according to each individual, there is no guarantee of your success or improvement level.

The author and publisher assume no responsibility for any of your actions, whether you use the information for positive or negative purposes.

Much of the information contained in this book is drawn from folklore collections, recipes given to the author from family, friends, customers, spiritual leaders, and healers over the span of a lifetime, recipes from 19th and 20th century formularies, historical accounts of African-based folk magic from slaves in the southern United States, objective evaluation of anthropological literature, and from the personal inspiration of the author. The information contained herein is subject to the interpretation of the author, and may or may not be entirely accurate.

As always, the advice of a competent professional should be sought.

The information contained in these pages is not meant as a

substitute for the advice of health or mental health professionals.

Readers should use discretion before performing any rituals.

The author is not liable, or in any way responsible, for any actions that readers may take as a result of the information contained in this book. The reader is encouraged to use the psalms responsibly

Matthew 6:9-13

King James Version

9 After this manner therefore pray ye: Our Father which art in heaven, Hallowed be thy name.

10 Thy kingdom come, Thy will be done in earth, as it is in heaven.

11 Give us this day our daily bread.

12 And forgive us our debts, as we forgive our debtors.

13 And lead us not into temptation, but deliver us from evil: For thine is the kingdom, and the power, and the glory, for ever. Amen.

THE PRAYER OF PROTECTION

By James Dillet Freeman (1912-2003)

The light of God surrounds me;

The love of God enfolds me;

The power of God protects me;

The presence of God watches over me;

Wherever I am, God is!

ACKNOWLEDGEMENTS

Thank you, my Heavenly Father-mother God, for granting me the wisdom, privilege and ability to write this book

Thank you, God for giving humanity the laws of success.

The human race has never been left stranded by the divine. Nature has left clues on what to do for you to become successful. Seek and you shall find.

Thank you, Reverend Dr. Samuel Sasu, Director of Center for Spiritual Awareness, West Africa.

Thank you, dear reader for your decision to read this book. Every day, in every way I see you soaring from one level of success to another, in the name of Jesus Christ.

FOREWORD

The book of psalms for several centuries has been called the perfect prayer book. Millions of people over the years have found spiritual comfort and great deliverance by unleashing the secret power hidden in pages of the psalms.

The psalms are a collection of 150 songs, prayers and decrees which make up the 19th book of the Old testament.

There is supernatural power that can be unleashed in the book of psalms when we apply its wisdom. It requires sincere faith and a pure heart to activate the divine power in the psalms.

It is advisable that you read this book carefully and practice the spiritual exercises as instructed. Be consistent and focused.

The prayers and decrees in the book of psalms have been used to win court cases, heal diseases, gain employment, increase business sales, overcome bad luck, protection from accidents, cure barrenness, overcome plans of enemies and attract good fortune.

The focus of this book is to teach you how to use psalms to attract more success into your life and business.

INTRODUCTION

This book is about using the psalms to manifest a successful life regardless of what circumstances around you may potray. It is your divine right to live a successful, happy and prosperous life. The decision is yours. Choose the best that life has to offer and you will that life.

It is an eye-opener to the secret mystical treasures and simple formulas which everyone can use to solve various everyday problems we come across in our search for a successful and happy life.

It is a book on practical spirituality for successful living. The ideas and spiritual exercises are very potent and easy to do.

Within the pages, you will find some affirmations that you can recite every morning and night. I encourage you to repeat the affirmations for 5 minutes, twice daily. Doing these exercises will help condition your mind to attract more success and prosperity as you go about your daily activities.

Study the entire book and do the spiritual exercises spread across its pages. Do it in faith.

Be persistent and have a positive mental attitude.

WHAT THIS BOOK WILL DO FOR YOU

This book is full of practical spiritual gems that will help you achieve success in the shortest possible time.

However, just reading this book will not do you any good — you must practice the rituals or formulas set forth in each of the psalms, and thus create for yourself a better life.

HOW TO GET THE MOST FROM THIS BOOK

Read it casually from start to finish. If something is not clear just proceed to the next page until you reach the end of the book.

You can now start all over again and carefully choose the psalms and formulas to work with. It requires your faith and persistence and you will begin to experience amazing results as you unleash the unlimited power hidden in the psalms.

I BELIEVE IN MY GOD-SELF

FOR SELF-CONFIDENCE- PSALM 23

I AM AND MY FATHER ARE ONE.

FORMULA 1

I AM BLESSED, FAVORED AND HAPPY.

Open your bible to psalm 23.
Stand before a mirror.
Carefully read the psalm in a prayerful mood. Take in 3 deep breaths. Look into your eyes in

the mirror and say this affirmation 33 times:

I BELIEVE IN THE POWER OF THE LIVING GOD. THAT POWER GIVES ME BOLDNESS NOW!

I AM IN TUNE WITH THE INFINITE.

FORMULA 2

I LIKE ME.

Open your bible to psalm 23. Relax your body and become still, physically and mentally for a few minutes.

Prayerfully and slowly read psalm 23. Stand erect with your two hands raised and spread upwards. Spread your legs apart, too.

Breathe in 21 times. After each breath, affirm these words:

I AM FILLED WITH ALL THE FULLNESS OF GOD.

After, saying these affirmations, remain still and silent for about 3 minutes before you go about your daily activities.

I BELIEVE IN THE POWER OF THE LIVING GOD.

FORMULA 3

I AM A CHILD GOD AND POSITIVELY SUCCESSFUL.

Open your bible to psalm 23.
Take in a deep breath and read

psalm 23 in faith. Repeat this process for 15 times. It means you will take in 15 deep breaths and read psalm 23, fifteen times.

Be still for a minute. Then affirm these words:

I BELIEVE IN THE POWER OF THE LIVING GOD.I BELIEVE! I BELIEVE!! I BELIEVE!!!

Remain still and calm for about a minute. Say your prayers for the day and thank God for the successes and victories awaiting you for the day.

SUCCESS IS MY DIVINE BIRTHRIGHT. I OWN IT.

FORMULA 4

THE CHRIST IN ME HELPS ME SUCCEED IN ALL THAT I DO.

Read psalm 23 carefully. Do this 3 times. Raise your hands above your head. Spread it out, with your fingers pointing to the sky. Spread your feet apart.

Take in 7 deep breaths. With every breath, declare this affirmation with full faith:

I AM FILLED WITH POWER.

Remain quiet and still for a minute and you can go about your business for the day. Do this exercise for 21 days and you will see yourself walking in supreme self-confidence.

I AM THE MANIFESTATION OF GOD AND I ONLY EXPERIENCE THE GOOD.

SUCCESS IN YOUR PROJECTS AND BUSINESS ENDEAVOURS- PSALM 5

MY BUSINESS IS A VERY POWERFUL MAGNET FOR SUCCESS AND PROSPERITY.

FORMULA 1

Open your bible to psalm 5. Take in 3 deep breaths. Read the psalm slowly and pay attention to every word and verse.

Take a sheet of paper and write down your personal or business projects. Make sure you are very specific.

Get a white or green candle. Consecrate the candle by rubbing it with blessed anointing olive oil. Light the candle.

Move the sheet of paper around the flames of the candle. Make sure that the paper doesn't get burnt. All we want to achieve is to get the candle fumes or smoke to blend with the sheet of paper in which your goals have been written.

Read the psalm the second time. Then, you can say the following prayer:

O DIVINE CHANANJAH, THE ALL-MERCIFUL GOD, PLEASE GUIDE AND PROSPER ME IN THIS PROJECT. LET YOUR EYES BE MY EYES. LET YOUR HANDS BE MY HANDS. MOVE WITH YOUR GRACE THROUGH MY FEET. LET YOUR WISDOM, GUIDE MY SPIRIT AND INTELLECT. MAY THIS PROJECT PROSPER FOR MY GOOD AND THE GOOD OF HUMANITY, IN THE NAME

OF OUR LORD, JESUS CHRIST.

Silently, thank God for answering your prayers. Be quiet before the presence of the Lord for about a minute. Move on with the activities of the day. Repeat this spiritual assignment for the next 21 days. You will definitely see results. Just believe!

I THINK, TALK, WALK, DREAM AND ACT SUCCESS

FORMULA 2

MY BUSINESS IS ALIVE, SUCCESSFUL AND PROSPEROUS.

If you have a business premises, you can use this formula.

Get a bowl or bucket of water. Add a teaspoon of cinnamon to the water. Add a pinch of salt and a teaspoon of coconut oil. Stir the water with your hand or a wooden ladle.

Read psalm 5 slowly and carefully into the water. Do this 3 times. Say the following prayer into the water:

O CHANAJAH, THE INFINITELY MERCIFUL GOD, I THANK YOU FOR YOUR GRACE AND COMPASSION TOWARDS ME AND THE WORKS OF MY HANDS. O MERCIFUL ONE, PLEASE BLESS THIS WATER AND ITS ADDITIVES. LET IT CANCEL AND ANNUL EVERY HEX, JINX, ENCHANTMENT, INCANTATION AND DIVINATION AGAINST MY

BUSINESS. LET YOUR PURE WHITE LIGHT FILL THE PREMISES OF MY BUSINESS AND THE OCCUPANTS.

O SUPREME GOD, SHOWER MY BUSINESS WITH A FLOOD OF HAPPY CUSTOMERS. MAY PROSPERITY AND GOOD FORTUNE VISIT MY BUSINESS LIKE A RUSHING RIVER FROM THE EAST, WEST, NORTH AND SOUTH. THANK YOU

FOR YOUR FINANCIAL BENEVOLENCE, IN THE NAME OF OUR LORD, JESUS CHRIST. SO BE IT. AMEN.

Get a new broom or mop that has never been used. Clean the floors of your business premises and watch your business prosper. Do this spiritual exercise, once a week. You will be amazed at the results.

Be quiet and still for a while. Go about your business with ease.

DIVINE LIFE AND WISDOM FLOWS THROUGH MY BUSINESS. I AM ALWAYS PROSPEROUS.

FORMULA 3

GOD PROSPERS MY BUSINESS NOW!

Get a bottle of original coconut oil. Place it on a table. Open the cover of the bottle. Read psalm 5 into the bottle of oil. Do this 3 times. Say the following prayer into the bottle of coconut oil:

GOD'S WEALTH FLOWS TO ME FROM ALL

DIRECTIONS IN AVALANCHES OF ABUNDANCE. I AM A CUSTOMER MAGNET. I ATTRACT THOUSANDS OF CUSTOMERS TO MY BUSINESS ON A DAILY BASIS. MY BUSINESS PROSPERS ME, MY STAFF AND ALL THE PEOPLE WHO USE OUR PRODUCTS AND SERVICES. THANK YOU GOD, FROM WHOM ALL BLESSINGS FLOW, IN

THE NAME OF OUR LORD, JESUS CHRIST.

Hold the bottle of oil in your hand and chant the name, JEHOVAH JIREH, for 21 times.

You can now use the oil to anoint yourself and your business premises. Do this once to thrice per week, for effective results.

MY BUSINESS
EXPERIENCES ONLY THE
GOOD.

FORMULA 4

MY BUSINESS IS A VERY POWERFUL MAGNET FOR TONS OF SATISFIED CUSTOMERS.

Before sunrise, take a bucket of water. Put in 7 drops of florida water, 3 teaspoon of coconut oil and 3 teaspoon of cinnamon powder or a teaspoon of cinnamon oil.

Stir the water with your hands or a wooden ladle. Allow the water to settle down.

Open your bible and read psalm 5 into the water. Read it slowly, with understanding. Read psalm 23 into the water, also. Say the following prayer:

O SUPREME GOD, THANK YOU FOR YOUR PROSPERING GRACE AND PRESENCE. I HUMBLY ASK THAT YOU USE THIS WATER AND ITS ADDITIVES AS A

CHANNEL OF YOUR BLESSINGS CONCERNING MY PERSONAL AND BUSINESS PROJECTS. LET YOUR STAR SHINE THROUGH THIS BUSINESS, MAKING ME AND MANY PEOPLE RICHER THAN BEFORE. LET THIS BUSINESS BE A CHANNEL OF GOOD TO THE WHOLE OF HUMANITY. I ASK FOR THESE AND MORE WHICH YOUR GRACE DESIRES TO GIVE ME, IN THE NAME OF

OUR LORD, JESUS CHRIST. SO BE IT. AMEN.

Then, take your bath with the water without drying your body with a towel. You can also sprinkle the water in your business premises or use it to wash the floor of your business premises or store.

Make sure that you wash the floor inwards into your premises since customers move inwards when they come to patronize. Wash the floor from your gate or door into your place of business activity.

EVERYDAY IN EVERYWAY, MY BUSINESS IS GROWING MORE PROSPEROUS.

BUSINESS BREAKTHROUGH - PSALM 8

I HAVE THE POWER TO MANIFEST WEALTH AND I USE IT NOW!

Open your bible to psalm 8 and read it slowly with understanding. Close your eyes as you take in 3 deep breaths.

Imagine a white door before you. See the words, "BUSINESS BREAKTHROUGH" written on the door in red colour. In your imagination, walk towards the door and turn the knob to open it. See yourself flooded with pure white light. Breathe in this light deeply.

Turn to your right and see another white door, with "business breakthrough" written across the door. Walk towards the door and open it. Breathe in the pure white light into your being.

From that position, make another turn to your right side and see another white door with the same words, "business breakthrough", written on it. Walk towards it and turn the knob. As you open it, breathe in the pure white light that radiates through the open door. Feel it flooding your being.

Then, make another right turn, and you will see the fourth door in your imagination. Walk towards and hold the door knob. As you open the door, you will be visited by a bright white light. Breathe in this bright light, deeply. Make sure there is a smile on your face.

Imagine yourself carrying out your business activities in the office or market place. See long queues of people coming for your products and services. See yourself, receiving large sums of money on a continuous basis. Feel the joy and excitement within you. Hear people thanking you for your products and services.

See yourself going to your bank to deposit large sums of money in your account. Feel the bag of money in your hands.

Pray the following prayer:

O RECHMIEL, THE GREAT AND STRONG GOD, I PRAISE THEE. I HUMBLY REQUEST FOR YOUR LOVE, GRACE AND MERCY TO BRING UNCOMMON, MASSIVE BUSINESS BREAKTHROUGH AND PROSPERITY. MAY MY BUSINESS TAKE FLIGHT LIKE AN EAGLE AND SOAR TO UNIMAGINABLE

FINANCIAL HEIGHTS AND PROGRESS. MAY I BE BLESSED WITH UNFATHOMABLE WISDOM AND FAVOR TO ATTRACT WEALTH FOR ME AND OTHERS. MAY I SIEZE MY OPPORTUNITIES OF GOLD WHEN THEY COME RUNNING MY WAY.

O SUPREME GOD, HELP ME TO BE AT THE RIGHT PLACE AT THE RIGHT TIME TO RECEIVE THE RICHES OF LIFE.

I ASK FOR ALL THESE AND MORE IN THE NAME AND THROUGH THE POWER OF JESUS CHRIST. AMEN.

Make your personal petitions to God and have a strong faith, that He will grant your request.

Do this spiritual exercise in the morning and evening for 3 days.

MY BUSINESS IS A MONEY MAGNET. IT PROSPERS EASILY

FORMULA 2

THE DIVINE SUBTANCE OF
THE UNIVERSE ATTRACTS
A CONTINUOS FLOOD OF

CUSTOMERS TO MY BUSINESS.

Get a bottle of water. Open the lid and read psalm into the water. Pray your specific desires into the water.

Hold the bottle of water in the palms of your hands. Visualize a ball of bright white light a foot above your head. Breathe in deeply this pure white ball of light and let it stop at your throat chakra.

Picture a pure white light radiating from your throat chakra and through the palms of your hands into the bottle of water. See bottle of water covered with the bright, white light. Say the following prayer:

DIVINE LIGHT AND LOVE BLESSES MY BUSINESS AND I EXPERIENCE SPEEDY GROWTH FOR THE GOOD

OF HUMANITY.

I AM POSITIVELY SUCCESSFUL IN ALL I THINK, SPEAK AND DO. EVERYTHING AND EVERYBODY PROSPERS ME NOW WITH A FLOWING RIVER OF CUSTOMERS AND UNLIMITED CASH. I AM RICH BEYOND MY WILDEST DREAMS. MONEY FLOWS TO ME LIKE A RAGING RIVER AND MY BUSINESS PROSPERS EASILY,

SPEEDILY AND FREELY. I GIVE THANKS TO GOD, THE ORIGINATOR OF INFINITE WEALTH.

I CHARGE THIS BOTTLE OF WATER WITH THESE WORDS OF POWER.

THANK YOU GOD, IN THE NAME OF JESUS CHRIST.

Pause, as you hold the bottle with your hands and picture your dreams as if they have manifested.

Chant OM, for 5 minutes with your attention on the bottle of water in your hands. The water will be charged with divine energy for supernatural business breakthroughs.

You can now drink the bottle of water in one sitting. You can also sprinkle your business environment with some of the water.

Be silent for a while as you imagine your business experiencing massive success.

THE PROSPERING POWER
OF CHRIST ATTRACTS
SUCCESS TO ME EASILY
AND SPEEDILY.

BREAK AWAY FROM THE BONDAGE OF POVERTY- PSALM 72

MY BUSINESS EASILY ATTRACT TONS OF SALES ON A DAILY BASIS.

POVERTY IS NOT REAL. PROSPERITY AND ABUNDANCE IS MY ONLY REALITY.

THE FORMULA

MY BUSINESS ATTRACTS GREAT MONEY MAKING OPPORTUNITIES.

Buy some cooked food or snacks and pray psalm 72 on them. You should buy enough to serve 10 to 21 people. Do this on the day of your birth. It may be Monday, Sunday, Wednesday, Thurday, Friday,

Tuesday, Saturday or Sunday. Choose your appropriate day.

Pray over the food or snacks with these words:

JEHOVAH AHA, PLEASE BLESS THIS FOOD ITEMS MEANT FOR THE POOR AND LESS PRIVILEDGED. LET IT BE CHARGED WITH YOUR LOVE AND LIGHT.

MAY IT BRING MORE LIFE, GOOD HEALTH AND STRENGTH TO WHOSOEVER EATS IT.

AS I REMEMBER THE LESS PRIVILEDGED, MAY YOU REMEMBER ME AND CROWN MY LIFE WITH YOUR WEALTH, HEALTH AND HAPPINESS.

MAY MY WEALTH BRING GOODWILL TO HUMANITY. MAY SILVER AND GOLD RUSH FROM EVERY DIRECTION INTO MY POCKET, PURSE, BAG AND BANK ACCOUNT.

I ASK FOR ALL THESE WITH THANKSGIVING, IN

THE NAME AND THROUGH THE POWER OF JESUS CHRIST. AMEN.

Take this food to the market place or wherever you find beggars and share it among them.

Do this for 7 weeks and you will experience a financial windfall in your personal and business life.

MONEY LOVES ME. I LOVE MONEY AND ALL ITS POSITIVE EXPERIENCES.

FORMULA

I AM A SUCCESSFUL BUSINESS PERSON.

Take a particular sum of money which you plan to give away, and put it on the table. Anoint the currency notes with blessed coconut oil.

Pray psalm 72 and luke 6:38 on the money. Pray on the money like this:

I BLESS ALL THE MONEY THAT I HAVE, GIVE AND RECEIVE.

AND, I RECEIVE A HUNDRED TIMES OF THE MONEY IN RETURN AS A REWARD FROM THE UNIVERSE. MONEY FLOWS TO ME FREELY AND EASILY NOW. I AM PROSPEROUS. I AM A MONEY MAGNET. I AM FINANCIALLY

INDEPENDENT. I AM! I AM!! I AM!!! AMEN.

Give the money away to the poor within 24 hours. Do this in the morning before noon.

Decree the following words for 108 times in the morning and evening for 7 days:

JEHOVAH JIREH PROSPERS ME NOW.

Declare the above words with feeling and faith.

Keep your spiritual exercise a secret. Do not share what you are doing with other people. The results will speak for itself.

Get ready for a flood of financial miracles.

MONEY IS MY FRIEND.

PSALM 78- FAVOR WITH KINGS, QUEENS AND INFLUENTIAL PEOPLE.

I AM COMFORTABLE BEING AROUND RICH, WEALTHY AND INFLUENTIAL PEOPLE.

FORMULA

Open your bible to psalm 78. Read it prayerfully in full faith.

Get a bottle of honey and read psalm 78 into it with the cover open. Do this spiritual exercise early in the morning, before sunrise.

Say the following prayer:

IN THE NAME OF JESUS CHRIST, FATHER GOD, BY YOUR MERCY, LET THE OIL OF FAVOUR FROM

YOUR THRONE OF GRACE, ENTER INTO THIS HONEY. MAY THIS HONEY BE TRANSFORMED INTO A BLESSED AND DIVINE HONEY. MAY THE HONEY BE CHARGED WITH THE SPIRIT OF FAVOUR, SUCCESS AND PROSPERITY. MAY I EXPERIENCE ONLY INFINITE GOOD, WHENEVER I USE THE HONEY TO PRAY.

O SUPREME GOD, MAY I BECOME A HUMAN MAGNET ATTRACTING KINGS, QUEENS, PRINCES, PRINCESSES AND INLUENTIAL PEOPLE. MAY THEY BLESS ME WITH THE RICHES OF LIFE.

MAY UNIVERSAL GOOD FLOW THROUGH ME FOR THE GOOD OF HUMANITY.

THANK YOU GOD, FOR UNLIMITED INFLUENCE, POWER AND PROSPERITY.

Say the above prayer three times as you hold the bottle of honey in your hands.

APPLICATION

Whenever you want go out for your business, you can put a drop of the honey in your hand and pray for a favourable outcome concerning your business deals. You can then lick the honey with your tongue.

You can also use the honey by putting a drop of it in the palm of your hand. Pray for your heart's desires and rub the honey into the palms of your hands. Touch your face with the palm of your hands as you say : THE FAVOR OF GOD IS UPON ME AND I AM FAVORED BY EVERYONE.

I AM SUPERNATURALLY FAVORED.

FORMULA 2

Get a bottle of honey and a tablespoon full of thyme. Pour the thyme in the honey. Mix the contents together. Open the cover of the bottle.

Read psalm 78 into the contents of the bottle. Pray like this:

O JEHOVAH GOD, LET YOUR DIVINE FINGER TOUCH THE CONTENTS OF THIS BOTTLE. MAY YOUR FACE SHINE UPON ME AND MY BUSINESS AND WORK AS I PRAY WITH THIS BLESSED HONEY.

I INVOKE THE WHITE LIGHT OF JEHOVAH GOD, TO ENTER INTO THIS HONEY AND THYME AND TRANSFORM IT INTO THE HONEY OF FAVOUR.

MAY KINGS AND OTHER INFLUENTIAL PEOPLE BE ATTRACTED TO ME AND MY PROJECTS. MAY THEY COMPETE WITH EACH OTHER TO GRANT ME FAVOURS AND ASSIST ME TO ACHIEVE MY GOALS,

SPEEDILY, EASILY AND PEACEFULLY.

I GIVE THANKS TO THE SUPREME GOD FOR GRANTING MY HEART'S DESIRES, IN THE NAME OF JESUS CHRIST.

APPLICATION

You can put a drop of the honey in the palm of your hand. Pray about your desire and lick the honey with your tongue.

You can also put a drop of the honey into a bucket water. Pray your desires into the water and take a soapless bath with it. Make sure that you do not dry your body with a towel or any fabric material.

You can also wash the floor of your office premises with a drop of the honey in a bucket of water. Allow the floor to dry naturally.

Repeat this exercise on a continuous basis until you experience your desired result.

I AM ONE WITH THE SPIRIT OF DIVINE FAVOR.

FORMULA 3

Get a bottle of olive oil and add 7 teaspoonful of honey into the oil. Shake the bottle very well.

Do a one-day fast from 6.00am to 6.00pm. Ask Jehovah God to have mercy on you. Avoid speaking to anybody during the period of the fast.

Break the fast with songs of praise and worship. Read psalm 78 into the contents of the bottle. Read it, three times.

Pray like this:

O JEHOVAH GOD, MAY YOUR FINGER OF MERCY TOUCH THIS OLIVE OIL AND HONEY. O BLESSED HOLY SPIRIT, PLEASE, BREATHE UPON THIS CONTENT AND TRANSFORM THE OIL INTO THE OIL OF FAVOUR AND SUCCESS.

WHENEVER I USE THIS OIL, MAY THE ANGELS OF FAVOUR AND GOODNESS FOLLOW ME WHEREVER I GO. MAY I ATTRACT DIVINE HELPERS FROM INFLUENTIAL, RICH AND FAMOUS PEOPLE OF THE EARTH. MAY GOOD FORTUNE SEEK ME OUT WHEREVER I GO.

MAY I BE SINGLED OUT BY GOD TO BE BLESSED BY THE GREAT AND SMALL. MAY I

EXPERIENCE OVERFLOWING GRACE IN ALL MY HUMAN AND ECONOMIC ACTIVITIES.

THANK YOU JEHOVAH GOD, FOR YOUR INFINITE BOUNTY AND LOVE, IN THE NAME OF JESUS CHRIST.

APPLICATION

Whenever you are going for an interview, business meeting or date, you can anoint your head, tongue, hands and feet with the oil.

Ask God to grant your desires. Sing some songs of praise and worship. Go about your business.

Please, repeat this spiritual exercise on a daily basis until you manifest your goals, dreams and desires.

You can also anoint your office and business environment with the oil. Make sure that you anoint the entrance and exit doors of your business.

The oil can be used to anoint your face and proposal, if you are bidding for a contract. Have faith in God as you bless your business document. Be confident that you will get a massive breakthrough and favour.

EVERYDAY, IN EVERYWAY, THE HOLY SPIRIT GUIDES ME INTO MY TRUE PLACE IN LIFE.

HOW TO RECEIVE INSTRUCTION FROM DREAMS AND VISIONS- PSALM 23

THE SPIRIT OF GOD REVEALS ALL I NEED TO KNOW THROUGH THE MEDIUM OF DREAMS AND VISIONS.

If you desire to receive instruction from God through dreams and visions, psalm 23 is very useful.

For this prayer to be effective, I advise you to undertake a 6.00am- 12.00noon or 6.00am - 6.00pm fast.

Take a bucket of water and pray psalm 23 into it, in full faith. After the prayer, call the name of God, JAH, 7 times into the water.

Pray this prayer :

O HEAVENLY FATHER, MAY YOUR NAME BE GLORIFIED. I THANK YOU FOR BEING THE ETERNAL REVEALER OF SECRETS.

O JAH, I HUMBLY ASK THAT YOU OPEN MY EYES OF UNDERSTANDING AND

GRANT ME WISDOM TO UNDERSTAND DREAMS AND VISIONS THAT I MAY DO WHAT IS PLEASING IN YOUR SIGHT.

O HOLY SPIRIT, LET ME UNDERSTAND THE DREAM LANGUAGE OF GOD. THANK YOU GOD FOR YOUR GRACE FOR REVELATIONS, IN THE NAME OF JESUS CHRIST. AMEN.

Invoke the name, JAH, 7 times into the water. Take your bath with the water, before sunrise.

You can repeat this spiritual exercise for 3 consecutive days.

I AM PROTECTED BY GOD

IF YOU ARE ABOUT TO BE ATTACKED- PSALM 18

I HIDE IN THE SECRET PLACE OF THE MOST HIGH GOD. I FIND PROTECTION UNDER HIS WINGS OF LIGHT.

If you are on a journey or at home and are about to be attacked by intruders or facing sudden danger, prayerfully, invoke the BLOOD OF JESUS, 7 times. Read psalm 18.

Then, say the prayer of protection as follows:

THE LIGHT OF GOD SURROUNDS ME.

THE LOVE OF GOD ENFOLDS ME.

THE POWER OF GOD PROTECTS ME.

THE PRESENCE OF GOD WATCHES OVER ME.

WHEREVER I AM, GOD IS,

AND, ALL IS WELL.

SO BE IT. AMEN.

Then, visualize yourself, surrounded by the pure white light of God.

I LOVE TO LOVE AND I AM LOVED IN RETURN.

HOW TO BE LOVED BY ALL- PSALM 47

I AM THE EMBODIMENT
OF LOVE.

Get a bottle of olive oil and 7 teaspoonful of honey or brown sugar. Add the honey or sugar into the oil.

Read psalm 47 into the bottle of oil. Do this 7 times. Pray that God will make you a channel of His love and a magnet of love to humanity. Shake the bottle to ensure that the contents mix together, properly.

Say this prayer:

I AM A LOVE BEING AND I ATTRACT ALL LOVING BEINGS TO ME.

EVERYDAY IN EVERY WAY, I LOVE AND I AM LOVED, UNCONDITIONALLY. THEREFORE, EVERYTHING AND EVERYBODY PROSPERS ME AND I PROSPER EVERYTHING AND EVERYBODY.

I THINK, SPEAK, FEEL, AND ACT IN LOVE TO EVERYONE I MEET OR RELATE WITH. I LOVE AND I RECEIVE BACK

LOVE, A THOUSAND TIMES MORE.

I AM THE EMBODIMENT OF LOVE.

I AM FILLED WITH DIVINE LOVE.

I AM. I AM. I AM. AMEN.

Place the bottle of oil on a window sill where sunlight can reach it. Leave it in that position for a whole day.

Anoint your head, face and chest with this oil before

sunrise, daily. Read and meditate on 1Corinthians 13.

Look at others with the eyes of love.

IN GOD I LIVE, MOVE AND HAVE MY EXPERIENCES. I AM DIVINELY SECURED.

TO BE PROTECTED FROM YOUR ENEMIES- PSALM 44.

FORMULA

Get a bottle of olive oil. Read psalm 44 into the oil for 7 days.

Say this prayer:

O SUPREME GOD, PLEASE HIDE UNDER THE WINGS OF YOUR DIVINE PROTECTION. LET YOUR

PRESENCE WATCH OVER ME.

LET THE SWORD OF JUDGEMENT KEEP MY ENEMIES A MILLION MILES FAR AWAY FROM ME, MY FAMILY, JOB AND HOME.

MAY DIVINE GOOD WRAP ITS ARMS AROUND ME, AT ALL TIMES. AMEN.

Anoint your head with the oil after you read psalm 91, every night before you sleep. Do this anointing for 21 days.

GOD ANSWERS MY PRAYERS, EVERYTIME.

QUICK ANSWERS TO PRAYERS- PSALMS 141

I ALWAYS RECEIVE QUICK ANSWERS TO MY PRAYERS.

Any time you want speedy answers to prayers, kindly read psalm 141, three times. Write your prayer petitions on a sheet of paper or card.

Make your prayer petitions to God. Have faith that God will grant your requests.

Place a glass of water on your prayer sheet or card. Hold the glass with both hands on the prayer card and chant HALLELUJAH, 21 times.

Maintain a minute of silence and drink the glass of water. Repeat this process, regularly until you receive the answer to your prayer.

GOD ANSWERS ME NOW.

OTHER BOOKS BY THE AUTHOR.

POWERS OF PSALMS FOR SUCCESS, PROSPERITY AND ABUNDANCE: How to attract money with hidden bible secrets.

POWERS OF PSALMS FOR HEALING:

A beginners guide to spiritual and chakra healing techniques for health and wellness.

AUTHOR

EDIN RINN is a practical spiritual writer and consultant, who has helped thousands of people to manifest more prosperity, abundance, good fortune, healings and untold blessings through his writings.

He loves travelling and speaking in spiritual seminars.

Manufactured by Amazon.ca
Bolton, ON